CHRISTOPHER HART

KIDS Draw ™

aNiMaLS

WATSON-GUPTILL PUBLICATIONS/
NEW YORK

No animals were harmed in the making of this book, and one was even fed.

For my daughters, Isabella and Francesca, two of the best artists I know.

Special thanks to Julie Mazur for suggesting this subject.

Senior Editor: Julie Mazur
Designer: Bob Fillie, Graphiti Design, Inc.
Production Manager: Hector Campbell
Text set in 12-pt Frutiger Roman

All drawings by Christopher Hart.

Cover art by Christopher Hart
Text copyright © 2003 Christopher Hart
Illustrations copyright © 2003 Christopher Hart

First published in 2003 by
Watson-Guptill Publications, an imprint of the Crown Publishing Group,
a division of Random House, Inc., New York
www.crownpublishing.com
www.watsonguptill.com

Library of Congress Cataloging-in-Publication Data
Hart, Christopher.
    Kids draw animals / Christopher Hart.
            p. cm. — (Kids draw)
Includes index.
Summary: Explores how to look at an animal, such as how it stands and
walks, and provides step-by-step instructions for drawing animals from
the jungle, savannah, farm, forest, and sea.
    ISBN 0-8230-2631-0
1. Animals in art—Juvenile literature. 2. Drawing—Technique—Juvenile
literature. [1. Animals in art. 2. Drawing—Technique.] I. Title. II. Series.
    NC780 .H26 2003
    743.6—dc21

                                        2002151435

Printed in China

First printing, 2003

8 /10 09

CONTENTS

Introduction 5

The Basics 6

HOW MOST MAMMALS STAND   TIPS AND TRICKS
HOW ANIMALS WALK

African Animals 10

PROUD LION   GIRAFFE
LEAPING LION   HIPPOPOTAMUS
GROWLING LION   ELEPHANTS: AFRICAN VERSUS INDIAN
GORILLA   AFRICAN ELEPHANT TAKING A DIRT BATH
OLD WORLD MONKEY   BABY AFRICAN ELEPHANT
RHINOCEROS   CHEETAH

Bears 24

GRIZZLY BEAR   POLAR BEAR
STANDING GRIZZLY   PANDA BEAR AND CUB
BLACK BEAR CUB

Horses 32

THE HORSE'S HEAD   3/4 VIEW
STANDING HORSE   HORSE DRINKING WATER
REARING HORSE

Birds 38

AMERICAN BALD EAGLE TOUCAN
OWL   PENGUIN
HAWK

Reptiles and Exotic Animals 44

CROCODILE   CAMEL
INDIAN COBRA   KANGAROO AND JOEY
GALAPAGOS TURTLE   HOPPING KANGAROO

Sea Creatures 52

DOLPHIN   SWORDFISH
SHARK   SEA LION AND PUP

Cute Critters and Pets 56

BEAVER   RACCOON
BUNNY RABBIT   DOG
PIG   WELSH SPRINGER SPANIEL
PIGLET   CAT

Index 64

INTRODUCTION

What's your favorite animal? Dogs? Cats? Horses? Or maybe it's penguins, or the humongous Galapagos turtle? Whatever it is, chances are this book will show you how to draw it!

We'll start by learning some basics about animals—how their bodies are put together, how they stand, how they walk. Then you'll draw all kinds of animals, from gorillas and grizzly bears to camels and crocodiles. Best of all, you won't be just copying, but really learning how to draw as you practice and have fun.

So is your pencil sharpened? Is your paper ready? Then let's start our journey through the wonderful world of animals. Just don't feed the lions!

THE BASICS

Let's start with a few basics. The more you know about how animals stand and move and walk, the better your drawings will be.

How Most Mammals Stand

Many of the animals you'll draw here are *mammals.* Mammals are animals like horses and dogs, who feed their babies with milk and have skin that is more or less covered with hair.

Most four-legged mammals have skeletons that are pretty much alike. Two that *don't* are the bear and the elephant. Believe it or not, their back legs are arranged more like people's!

This is how a human would look if standing like a horse. Most four-legged mammals stand on their "fingers" and "toes"—not on their "hands" and "feet," as you might think.

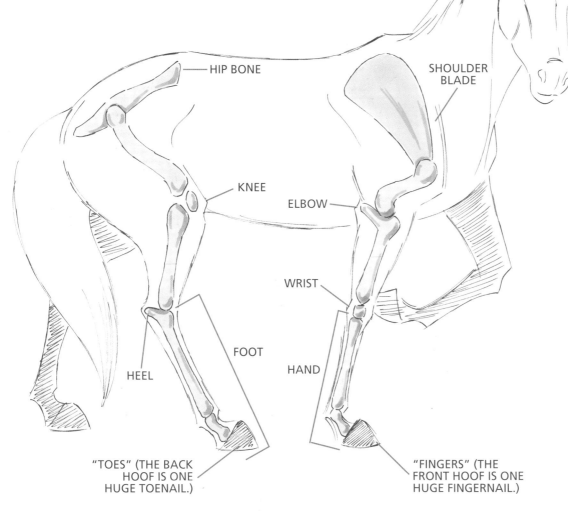

HIP BONE

SHOULDER BLADE

KNEE

ELBOW

WRIST

FOOT

HAND

HEEL

"TOES" (THE BACK HOOF IS ONE HUGE TOENAIL.)

"FINGERS" (THE FRONT HOOF IS ONE HUGE FINGERNAIL.)

Many other types of mammals have this same basic skeleton. See how the skeleton creates "bumps" in each animal's outline?

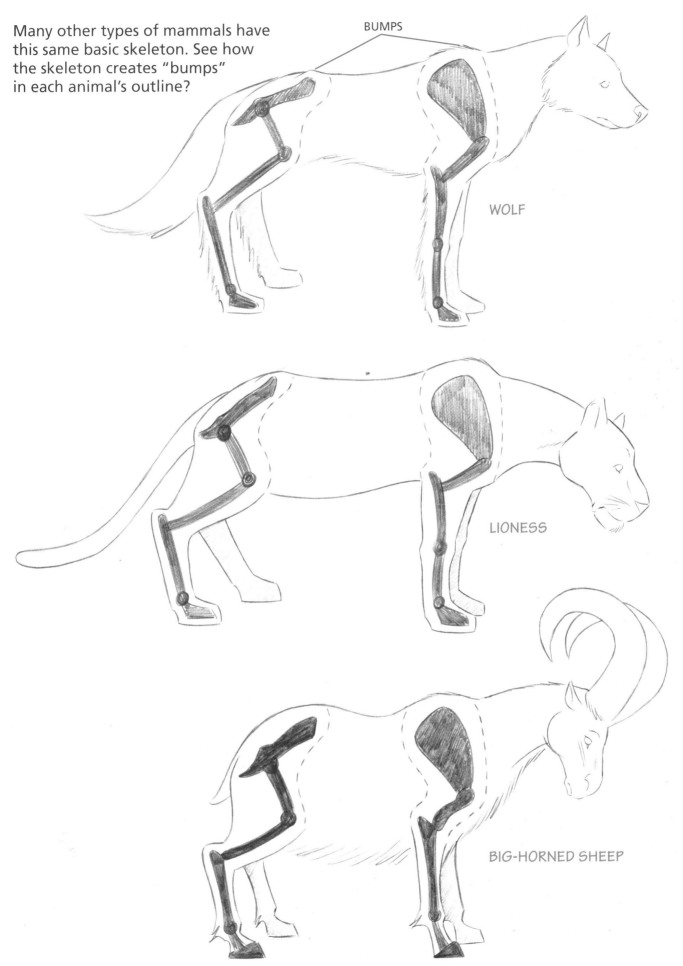

BUMPS

WOLF

LIONESS

BIG-HORNED SHEEP

How Animals Walk

Animals with four legs walk in very specific ways.

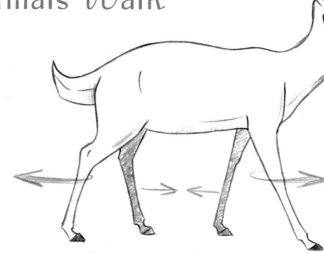

RIGHT
The legs nearer to us are spread apart. The legs farther away (the shaded ones) are closer together.

RIGHT
This is also correct. The legs nearer to us are now closer together. The legs farther away (the shaded ones) are farther apart.

WRONG!
Animals never walk like this. If they did, they would tip over whenever they lifted their legs to take a step!

Here are a few tips for making your drawings look more realistic.

Make the nearer legs a little longer than the farther legs. This is because of a rule in art called perspective. Perspective says that things closer to us look larger than things farther away.

Shade in the arms and legs that are farther away. This helps the closer ones stand out.

To draw an animal on all fours, draw a box around the feet. This will keep the pose lined up right. (See how the front of the box is wider than the back? This is because of perspective.)

AFRICAN ANIMALS

I t's time for the fun stuff—drawing animals! Let's start in the wild jungles and savannas of Africa.

Proud Lion

The lion has a massive skull. The forehead is small and the chin is big. Its forearms are thick and powerful. To make the lion look proud, push out its chest.

LONG "TEAR STAIN"

Leaping Lion

Here's another lion. Even though its neck is under its mane, you should still draw it. This will help you get the right length for the neck. Just erase it after you've added the mane.

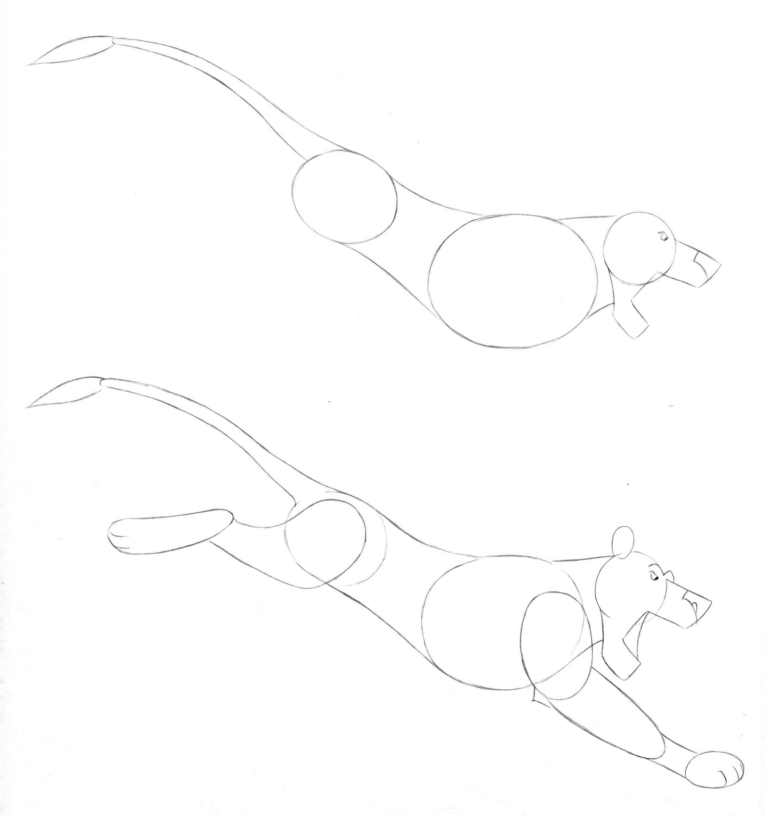

Growling Lion

Is there anything scarier than a growling lion? The eyes get beady and narrow...the forehead creases... the nose crinkles...the teeth are bared.... Yikes!

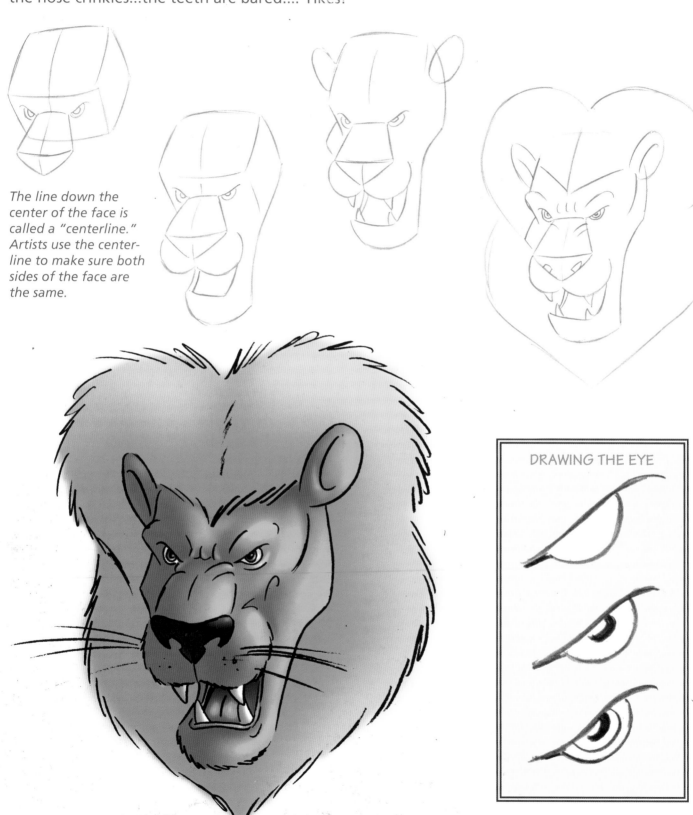

The line down the center of the face is called a "centerline." Artists use the centerline to make sure both sides of the face are the same.

DRAWING THE EYE

Gorilla

Gorillas are strong but they can also be very gentle, especially when caring for their young. Every group of gorillas has a male who's in charge. He's called the "silverback."

Use curving lines to draw the body.

Old World Monkey

The monkey's arms are longer than its legs. It also has long, thin fingers and toes for holding onto vines.

Draw the tail early on. If you wait too long, you might run out of room on the paper!

Rhinoceros

Rhinos have heads that look like saddles, bulky bodies, and tiny legs. Even though rhinos are huge, they can charge their enemies at very high speeds.

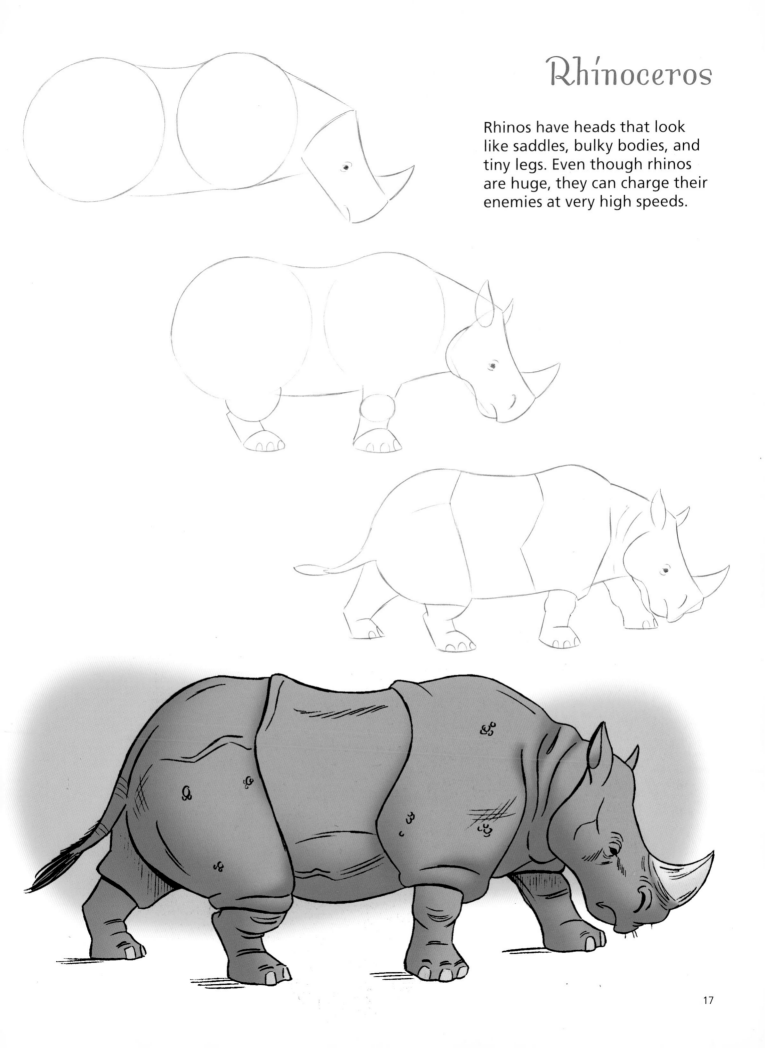

Giraffe

As everyone knows, giraffes have long necks. They also have huge chests and shoulders, but tiny hips.

The coat has big patches of brownish-red with tiny bands of white in between.

Hippopotamus

The hippo's body is easy to draw, but its head is tricky. To make it easier, draw the head in two parts. Then bring them together to finish.

Elephants: African Versus Indian

Let's look at the differences between these two types of elephants.

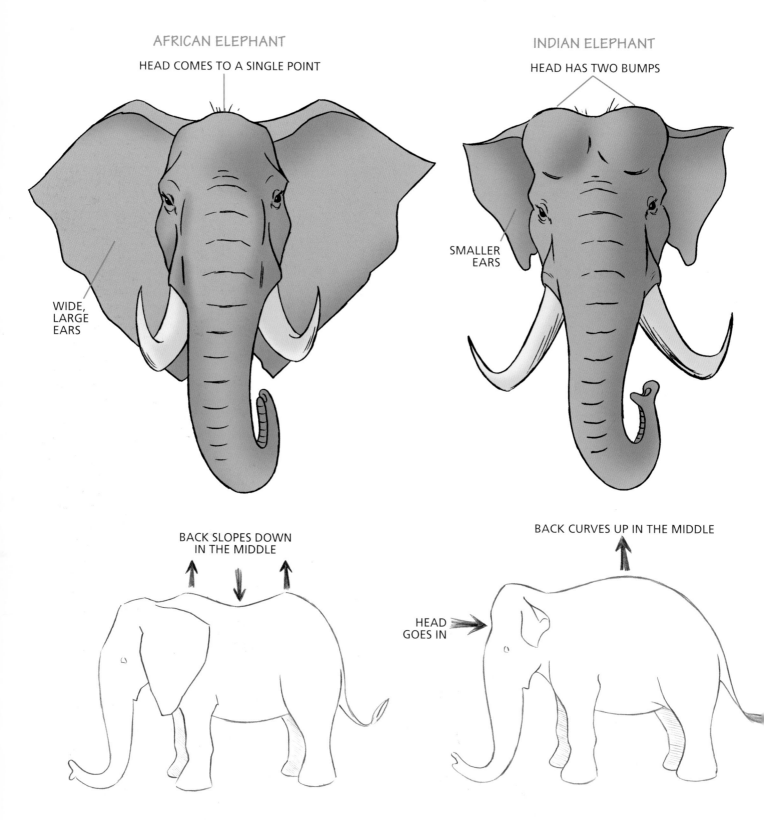

AFRICAN ELEPHANT
HEAD COMES TO A SINGLE POINT

INDIAN ELEPHANT
HEAD HAS TWO BUMPS

WIDE, LARGE EARS

SMALLER EARS

BACK SLOPES DOWN IN THE MIDDLE

BACK CURVES UP IN THE MIDDLE

HEAD GOES IN

African Elephant Taking a Dirt Bath

African elephants are my favorite. Here's one flinging dirt on itself to get rid of insects and pests.

Baby African Elephant

Baby elephants have big foreheads and even bigger ears. Their bodies are round, but thinner than an adult's. This makes their legs look longer and less sturdy. And their feet look too big for their bodies, just as puppies have big paws.

Cheetah

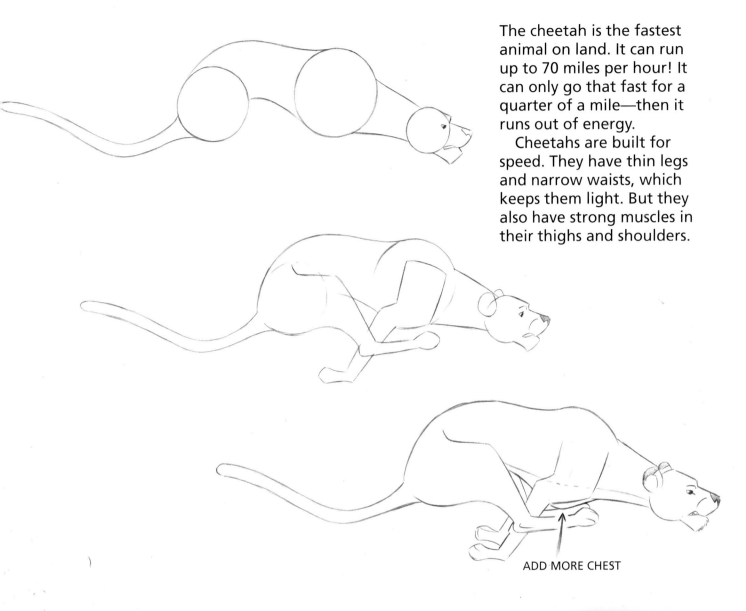

The cheetah is the fastest animal on land. It can run up to 70 miles per hour! It can only go that fast for a quarter of a mile—then it runs out of energy.

Cheetahs are built for speed. They have thin legs and narrow waists, which keeps them light. But they also have strong muscles in their thighs and shoulders.

ADD MORE CHEST

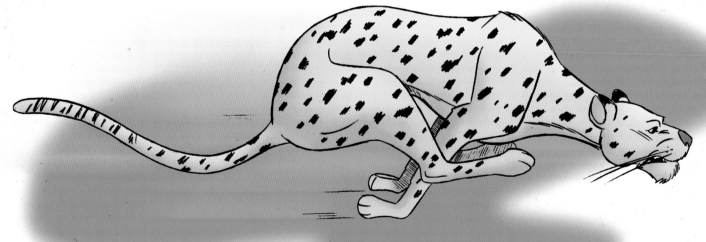

BEARS

Bears are very popular animals. They're the stars of cartoons and picture books. They're on candy and cereal boxes. And, of course, teddy bears make the best cuddle dolls ever! But not all bears are alike. Let's draw a few kinds.

Grizzly Bear

Grizzlies are massive animals with big bottoms. Their paws are thin but their legs and arms are thick and powerful. (In this pose you can't see the tail.)

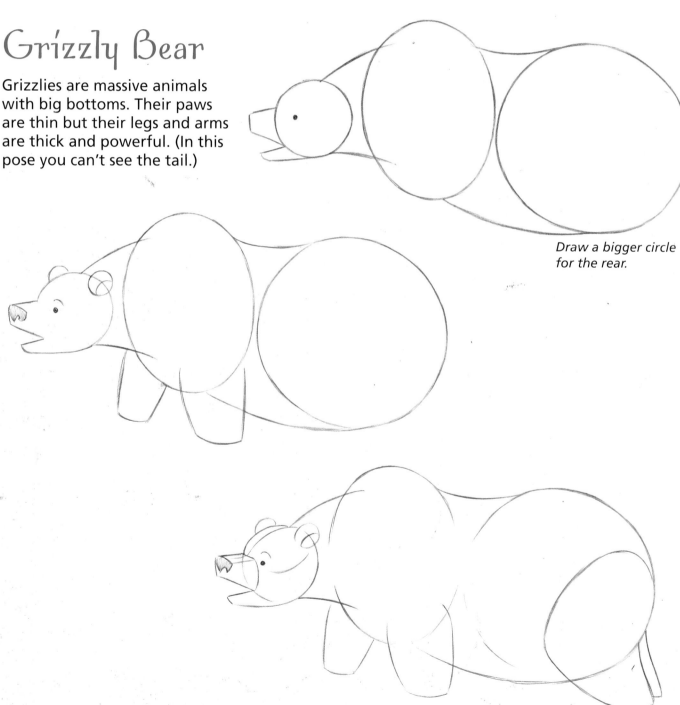

Draw a bigger circle for the rear.

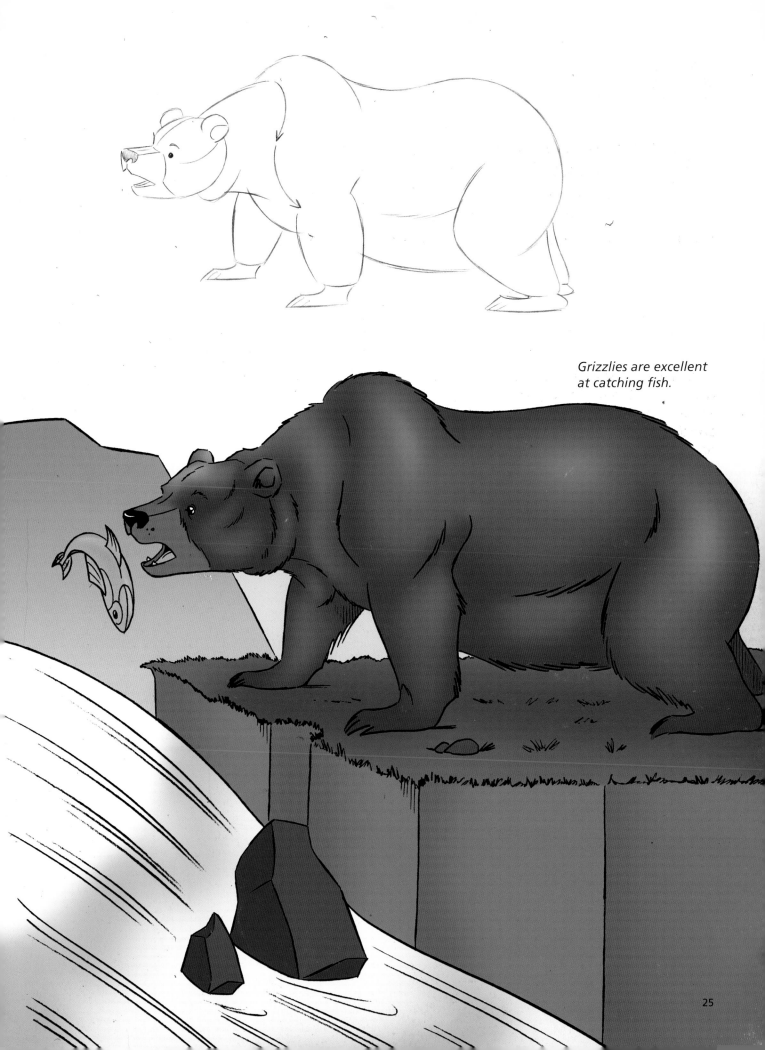

Grizzlies are excellent at catching fish.

Standing Grizzly

Bears can also stand on
two legs, like humans.

Black Bear Cub

Baby bears have heads that are big for their bodies. They have poochy little tummies and small chests. Their snouts are short, and they've got big eyes. This cub is a black bear. Black bears are the most common type of bear. They are smaller than grizzlies.

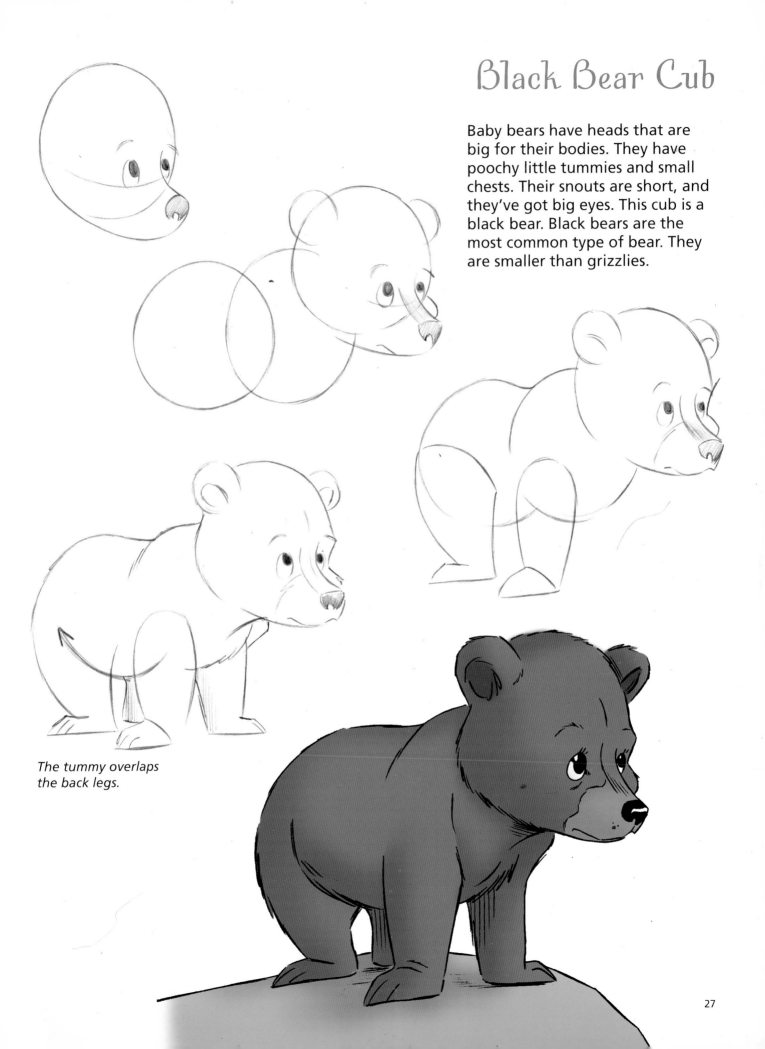

The tummy overlaps the back legs.

Polar Bear

Polar bears are great hunters that live in cold
northern climates. To catch their prey, they have
to get into the freezing cold waters of the Arctic.
So it's no surprise that they are excellent swimmers.

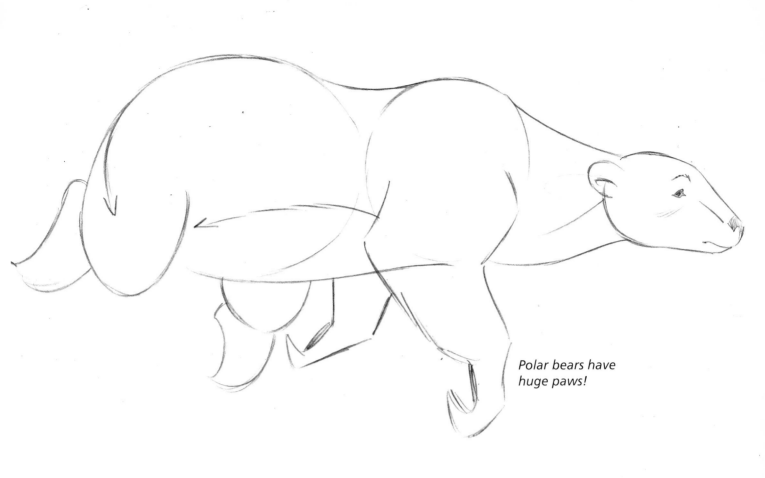

Polar bears have huge paws!

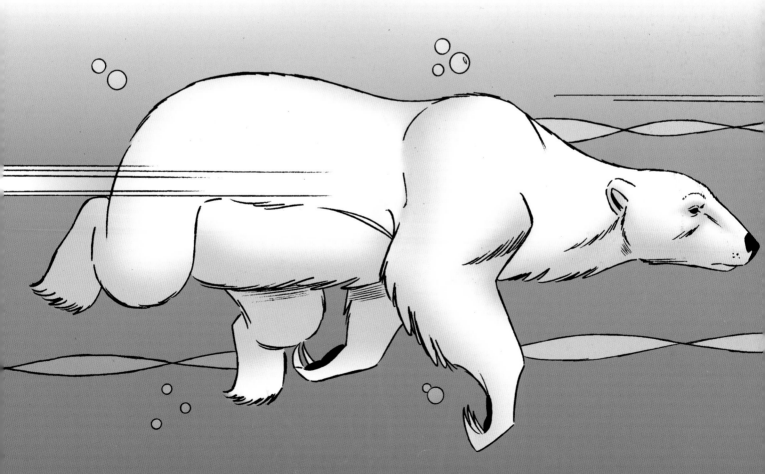

Panda Bear and Cub

Here's a playful panda mom and her cub. The pandas' distinctive black and white markings are what make them so popular. Outside of zoos, these bears can only be found in China. Sadly, this beautiful bear is an endangered species.

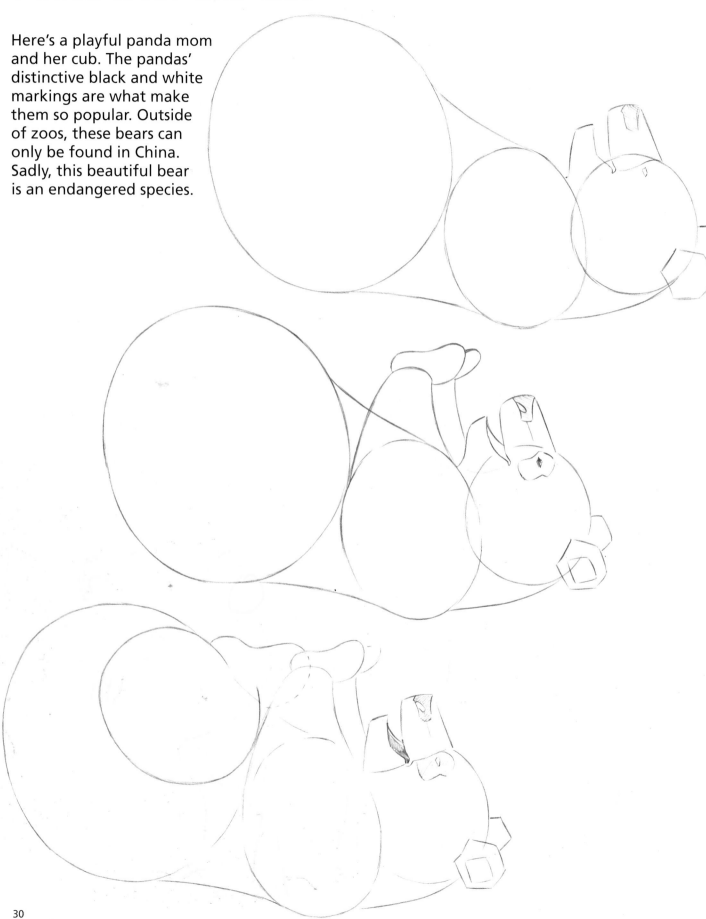

HORSES

Artists love to paint horses because they are such strong, graceful animals. Let's start with the head, then try a few poses.

The Horse's Head

The horse's head is very wide at the jaw and thin at the nose.

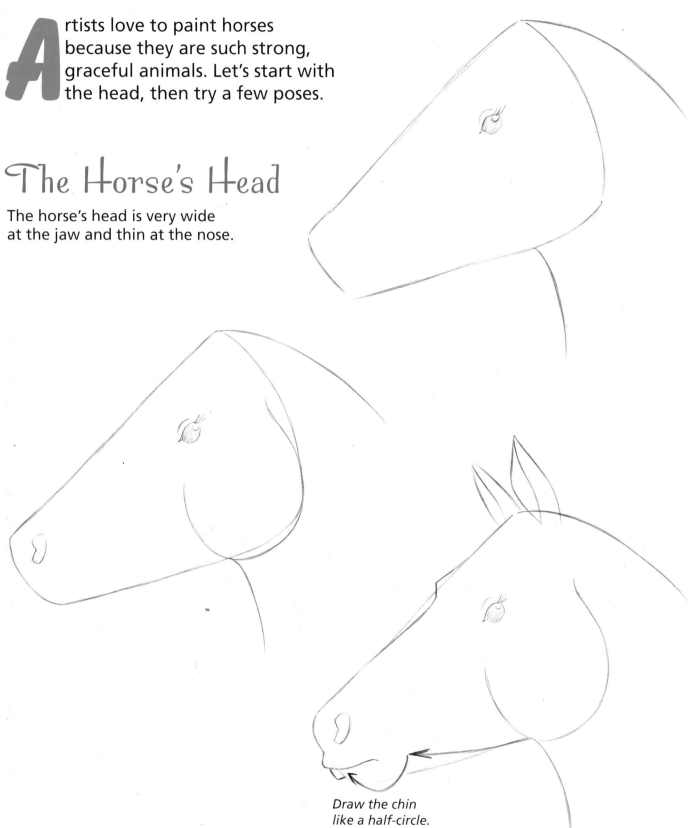

Draw the chin like a half-circle.

Here's how to draw the horse's eye with "shines." This makes it glisten and look alive. See how there's hardly any "white" showing? This is how most animals' eyes are.

Standing Horse

Horses are proud, mighty creatures. Sometimes I watch the horses near my house. I always try to remember how they look so I can draw them later.

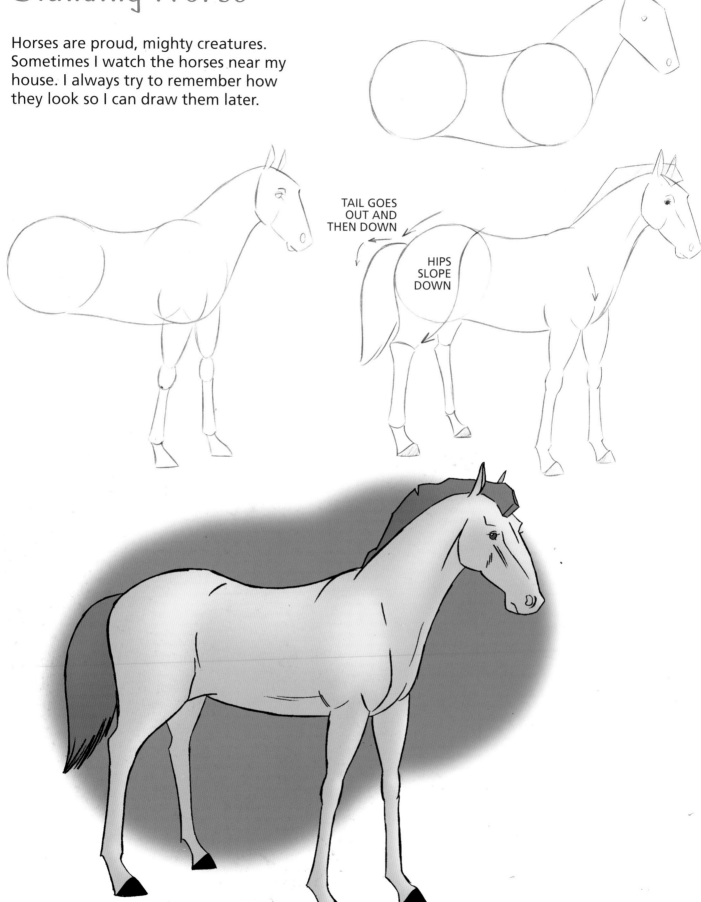

TAIL GOES OUT AND THEN DOWN

HIPS SLOPE DOWN

Rearing Horse

When a horse is spooked—by a bee, for example—it rises up on its two rear legs and waves its forearms.

3/4 View

The first two drawings you did were "side views," as if you were looking at the horse from one side. Now let's try a 3/4 view. This is something between a front view and a side view.

Notice how the body is shorter in this view? This is because the horse's front is hiding part of its rear.

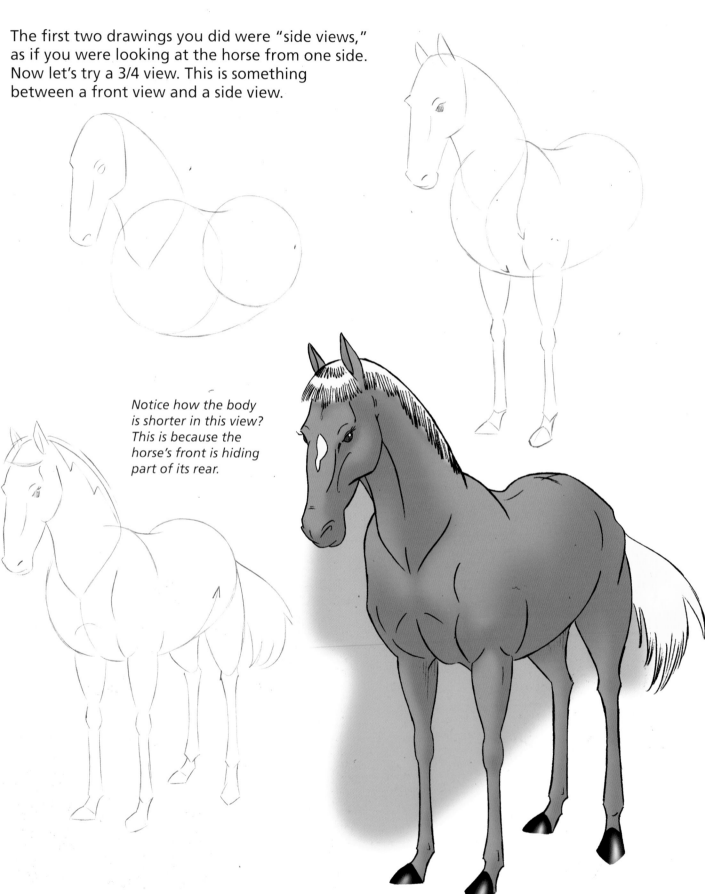

Horse Drinking Water

The horse's neck is so long it can drop its head to drink water without bending over. The horse is a very muscular, lean animal. You can see the outlines of bones and muscles underneath its skin.

HIPS SLOPE
DOWN

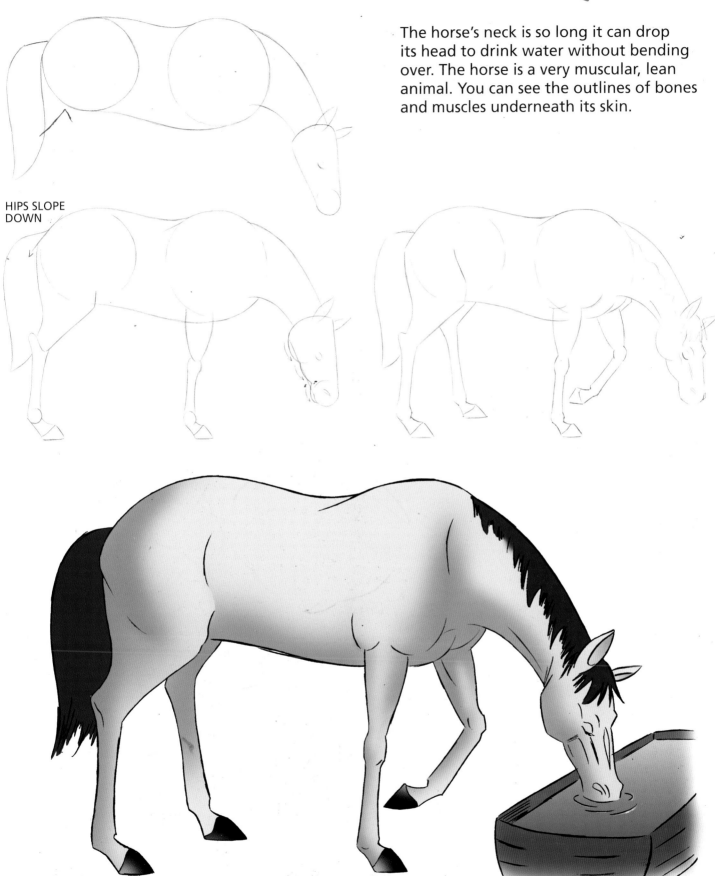

BIRDS

Some birds fly, others swim. Some hunt during the day, others hunt only at night. Some live in the tropics, others live in the Arctic Circle. Wherever they live, whatever they do, birds continue to fascinate us.

American Bald Eagle

Look at the eagle's sharp, hooked beak—this tells you right away that it's a hunter. Eagles have amazing vision. This is where the term "eagle eye" comes from. They use their sharp claws to snatch fish from lakes and streams.

Owl

Owls sleep during the day and are active at night. Their large eyes help them see in the dark. Owls might make you think of haunted houses, but they're actually very helpful animals. They eat unwanted pests, such as mice. The beak is small but it's hooked. This tells us the owl is a hunter.

Hawk

The hawk's hooked beak tells you it's a hunter, like the owl and the eagle.

Toucan

The toucan is a lively, friendly looking bird that lives in the tropics. Its beak is almost as long as its body. The upper beak is much thicker than the lower beak. And check out those stripes!

Penguin

Penguins have plump bodies, small heads, and sharp beaks. You might be surprised to learn that their wings are really quite long. Baby penguins look furry, unlike their smooth parents.

REPTILES AND EXOTIC ANIMALS

These are the cool animals that most American kids don't see around much. This might make them seem harder to draw. But with a little practice, even a Galapagos turtle is easy!

Crocodile

The "croc"'s body is simple to draw—it's just one long shape. But the head is kind of tricky. Here are three tips to remember:

1. The eyes bulge up above the forehead.

2. The tip of the nose gets bigger.

3. The mouth starts up high, near the eye.

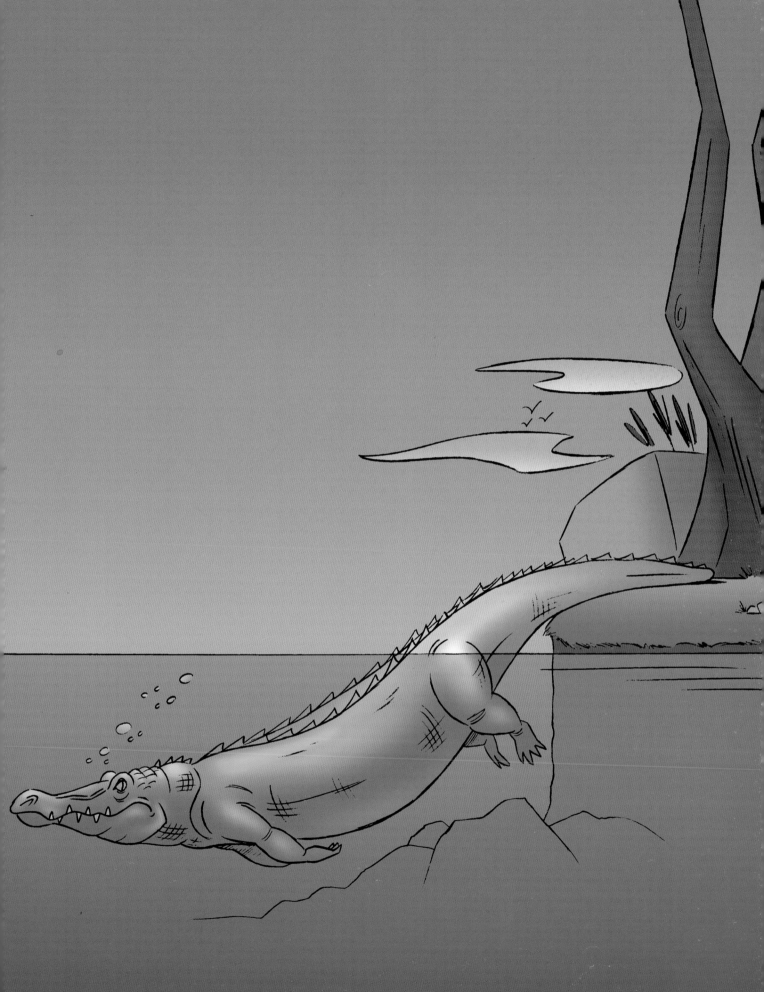

Indian Cobra

This snake can spit poison into its enemies' eyes, blinding them on the spot. Check out the cobra's "hood." And have fun with those markings!

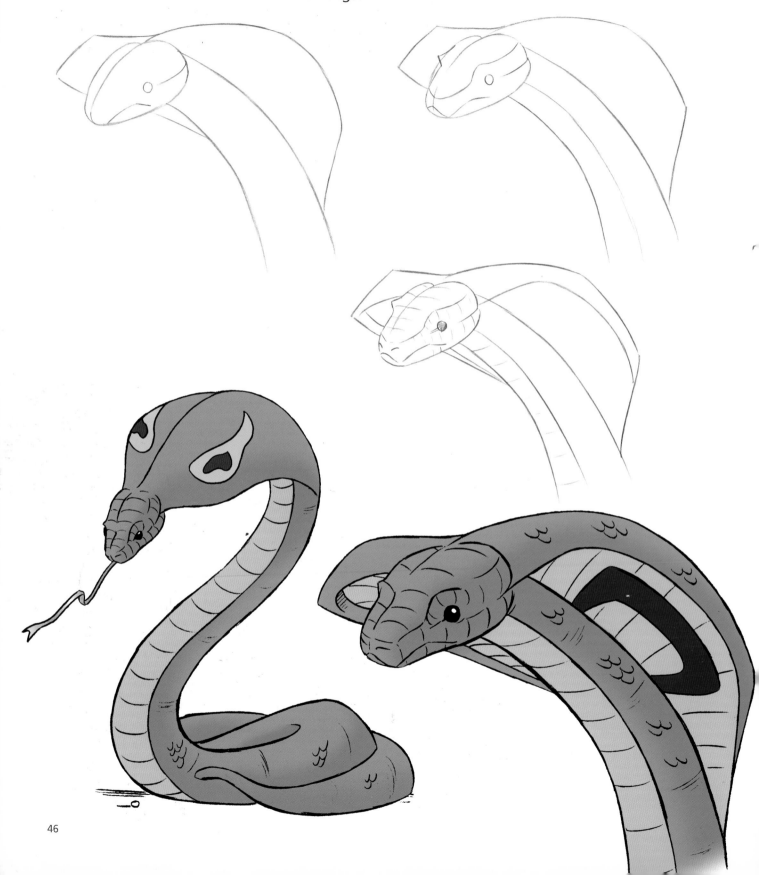

Galapagos Turtle

The Galapagos turtle isn't actually a turtle at all, but a *tortoise*. Its flat, elephant-like feet tell you that this big fella can't swim. It's strictly a land animal. It's got a tiny head and huge arms, which it uses not only to walk, but to dig. The Galapagos can weigh more than 500 pounds!

Camel

The most famous thing about the camel is its hump. Many people think the camel stores water in its hump, but this isn't true. The hump is really a big mound of fatty tissue. When food is hard to find in the hot, dry desert, the camel uses this fat for energy.

Kangaroo and Joey

Here's one of the "wonders from Down Under" —Australia, that is. The baby kangaroo is called a "joey."

Kangaroos have long tails, strong legs, and tiny arms. When they're not hopping, their long feet lie flat on the ground.

Hopping Kangaroo

When the kangaroo hops, it pushes off of the balls of its feet, much like the way a person runs.

The kangaroo pushes off of its toes, just like we do when we run.

SEA CREATURES

Get your scuba gear on, because we're about to take a dive! There are some cool, some cute, and even some terrifying creatures that live in the ocean.

Dolphin

The friendly dolphin is easy to draw. It's got a large, rounded forehead and a rounded body with stiff flippers. Its mouth makes it look like it's smiling.

Shark

The shark has many rows of small, razor-sharp teeth. (You can't see them all in this pose.) In case you didn't know, that famous fin on its back is called a "dorsal fin."

Here's a tip for drawing the eyes of sharks or any other fish: Never show eyelids. Leave the eyes wide open.

Swordfish

The swordfish is a deepwater fish. It is long and leaner than the shark, with long, graceful fins. Its head goes gradually into the shape of a sword—try not to make it look as if a sword has just been "stuck" onto its face.

Sea Lion and Pup

The head of a sea lion looks a lot like the head of a dog, but without the long ears. Its neck is wide and its chest is proud. A baby sea lion is called a "pup."

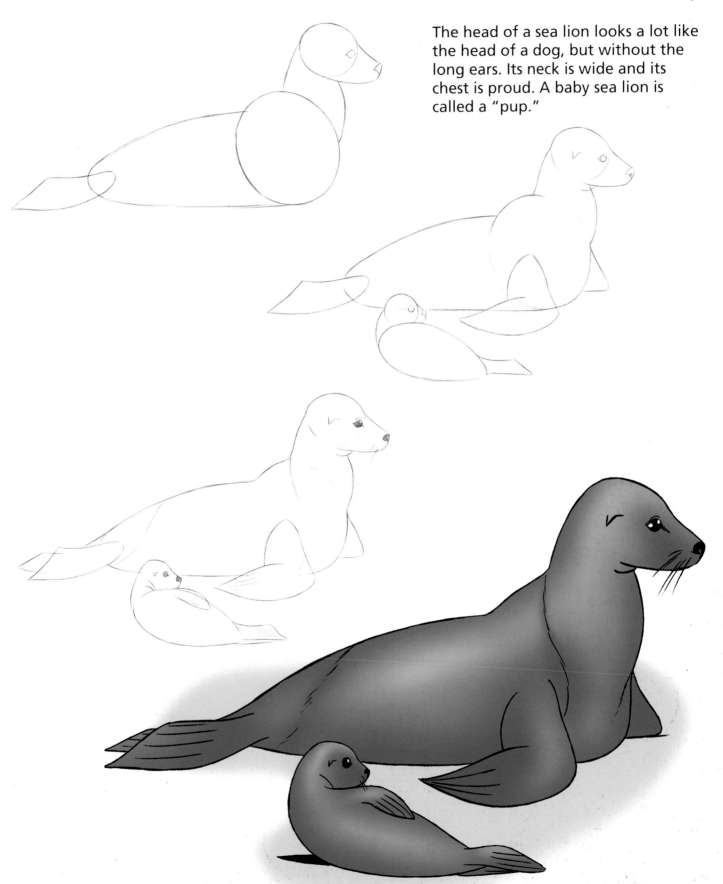

CUTE CRITTERS AND PETS

This book just wouldn't be complete without a few cute critters—and of course our best friends, cats and dogs!

Beaver

This little fella is all work and no play—a few beavers can build a dam in no time. Beavers have big noses and small eyes. They also have chubby arms and legs, but skinny hands and feet. Beavers are so cute, it's hard to believe they're in the rodent family!

Bunny Rabbit

The bunny rabbit always sits with its back arched. Can you guess why? It's all coiled up so it can jump at the slightest danger.

TAIL
TURNS UP

Pig

Did you know that pigs are very smart animals? You might also be amazed at how big a pig's body can get. Some weigh up to 400 pounds! But no matter how large a pig is, its legs are always tiny.

Piglet

A piglet's belly looks higher off the ground than an adult's. Its legs are long compared to its body. And its ears are quite big.

Raccoon

Raccoons are always getting into things. If I leave my garage door open at night, I can be sure the trash bags will be torn open by morning. And we all know who did it!

Raccoons have wide faces and pointy noses. Their "bandit" eye-masks and striped tails make them easy to spot.

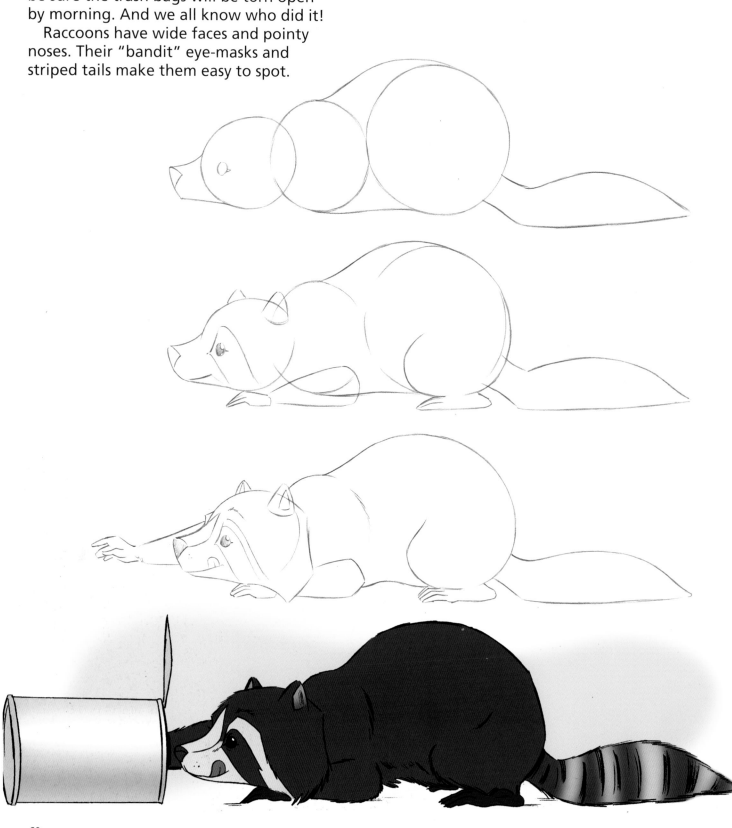

Dog

I couldn't create a book about animals and leave out "man's best friend," could I? Here's one of the most popular breeds: the lovable Labrador retriever. Other types of dogs sit this same way.

Welsh Springer Spaniel

This is my dog, Rusty. He's a Welsh springer spaniel and has rust-colored markings. Rusty is always energetic, devoted to his family, and loves children. I'm glad he's part of our family.

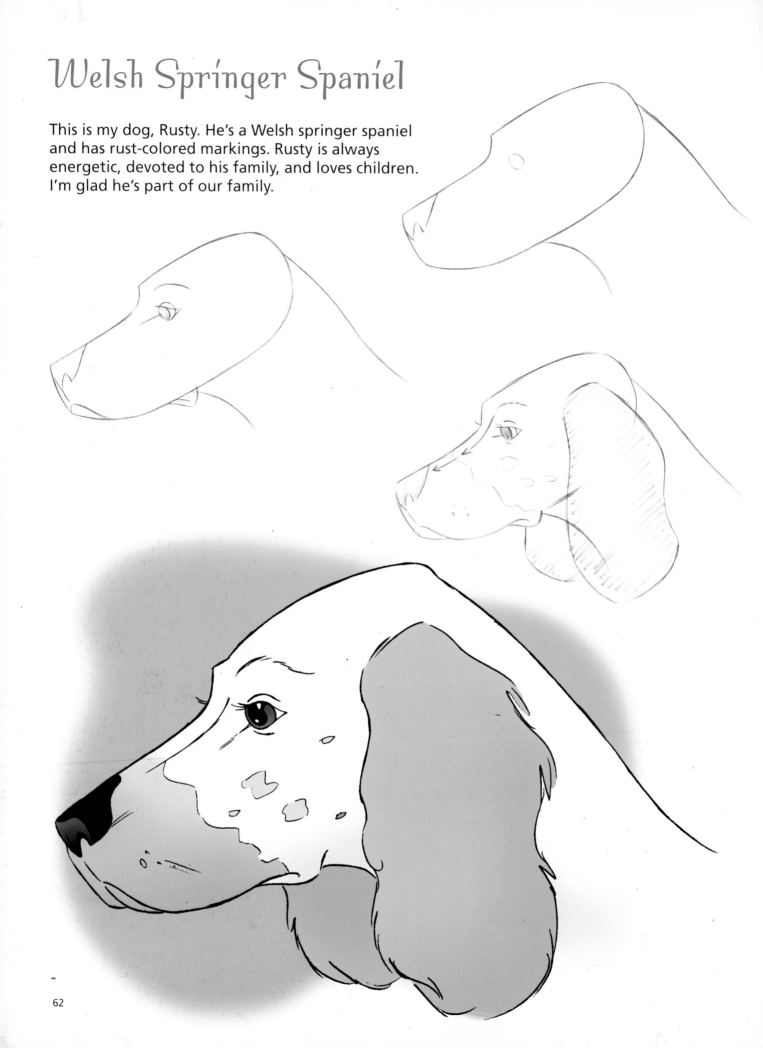

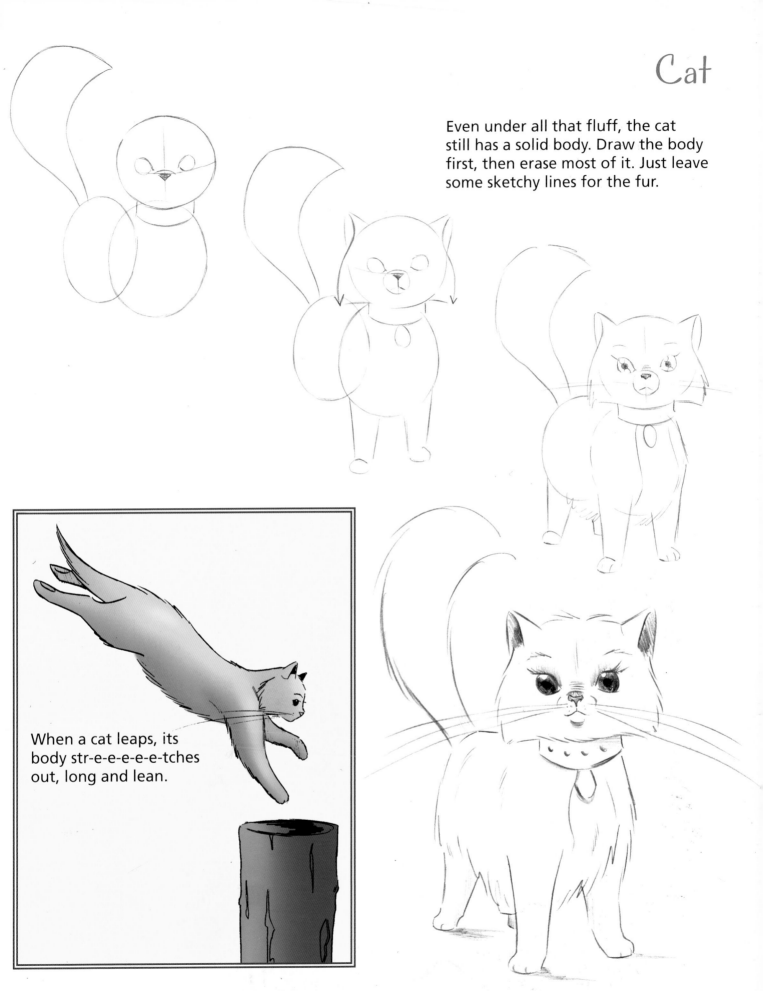

Even under all that fluff, the cat still has a solid body. Draw the body first, then erase most of it. Just leave some sketchy lines for the fur.

When a cat leaps, its body str-e-e-e-e-e-tches out, long and lean.

Index

African animals, 10–23
African elephant
    baby, 22
    differences between Indian
    and, 20
    taking a dirt bath, 21
American bald eagle, 38–39
animals. *See also* mammals
    on all fours, 9
    basics, 6–9
    walking, 8, 9

baby animals
baby African elephant, 22
baby kangaroo (joey), 50
baby penguin, 43
black bear cub, 27
    panda bear cub, 31
    piglet, 59
    sea lion pup, 55
bears, 24–31. *See also specific types*
black bear cub, 27
beaver, 56
big-horned sheep, 7
birds, 38–43. *See also specific types*
bunny rabbit, 57
    jumping, 9

camel, 48–49
cat
    leaping, 63
    standing, 63
    walking, 9
centerline, 14
cheetah, 23
crocodile, 44–45

dogs
    sitting Labrador retriever, 61
    Welsh springer spaniel, 62
dolphin, 52

elephant
    baby African, 22
    differences between African and
    Indian, 20
    standing on all fours, 9
eyes, drawing
    crocodile, 44
    horse, 33
    lion, 14
    long "tear stain" in lion's, 10

shark, 53
    "shines" in, 33

Galapagos turtle, 47
giraffe, 18
gorilla, 15
grizzly bear, 24–25
    standing, 26

hawk, 41
hippopotamus, 19
horse, 32–37
    drinking water, 37
    eyes, 33
    head, 32
    rearing, 35
    skeleton, 6
    standing, 6, 34
    3/4 view, 36

Indian cobra, 46

kangaroo
    hopping, 51
    and joey, 50

lion
    eyes, 10, 14
    growling, 14
    leaping, 12–13
lioness skeleton, 7
    proud, 10–11

mammals. *See also* animals
    definition of, 6
    skeletons of, 6–7
    standing, 6–7, 9
monkey, Old World, 16

Old World monkey, 16
owl, 40

panda bear, 30
    and cub, 31
penguin, 43
pig, 58
    baby (piglet), 59
polar bear, 28–29

raccoon, 60
reptiles, 44–47. *See also specific
    animals*
rhinoceros, 17

sea creatures, 52–55. *See also
    specific animals*
sea lion and pup, 55
shark, 53
skeletons
    big-horned sheep, 7
    horse, 6
    lioness, 7
    wolf, 7
swordfish, 54

tips and tricks, 9
tortoise, 47
toucan, 42

wolf, 7